SCHOLASTIC

READ & RESPOND

Helping children discover the pleasure and power of reading

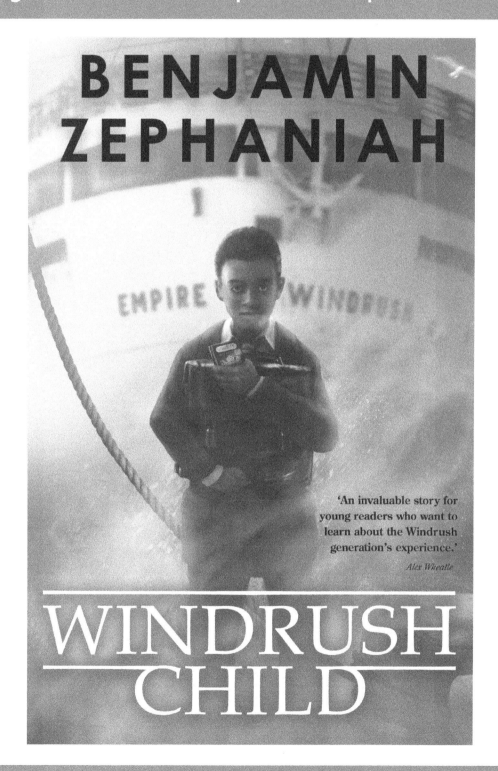

BENJAMIN ZEPHANIAH

'An invaluable story for young readers who want to learn about the Windrush generation's experience.'
Alex Wheatle

WINDRUSH CHILD

FOR AGES 9–11

Published in the UK by Scholastic, 2022

Book End, Range Road, Witney, Oxfordshire, OX29 0YD

Scholastic Ireland, 89E Lagan Road, Dublin Industrial Estate, Glasnevin, Dublin, D11 HP5F

SCHOLASTIC and associated logos are trademarks and/or registered trademarks of Scholastic Inc.

www.scholastic.co.uk

© 2022 Scholastic Limited

1 2 3 4 5 6 7 8 9 2 3 4 5 6 7 8 9 0 1

A CIP catalogue record for this book is available from the British Library.
ISBN 978-0702-30859-8

Printed and bound by Ashford Colour Press
Paper made from wood grown in sustainable forests and other controlled sources.

Extracts from *The National Curriculum in England, English Programme of Study* © Crown Copyright. Reproduced under the terms of the Open Government Licence (OGL). http://www.nationalarchives.gov.uk/doc/open-government-licence/version/3

Authors Sally Burt and Debbie Ridgard
Editorial team Rachel Morgan, Sarah Sodhi, Jane Cotter and Julia Roberts
Series designer Dipa Mistry
Typesetter QBS Learning
Cover illustrations Greg Straight/Illustration X
Illustrator Carlo Molinari
Photographs page 8: Benjamin Zephaniah, Adrian Pope; page 18: HMT *Empire Windrush*, Royal Navy official photographer, Public domain, via Wikimedia Commons

Acknowledgements
The publishers gratefully acknowledge permission to reproduce the following material:
Scholastic Children's Books for the use of the text extracts and cover from *Windrush Child* written by Benjamin Zephaniah.
Every effort has been made to trace copyright holders for the works reproduced in this book, and the publishers apologise for any inadvertent omissions.

For supporting online resources go to:
www.scholastic.co.uk/read-and-respond/books/windrush-child/online-resources
Access key: Return

CONTENTS ▽

How to use Read & Respond in your classroom...

Read & Respond provides teaching ideas related to a specific well-loved children's book. Each Read & Respond book is divided into the following sections:

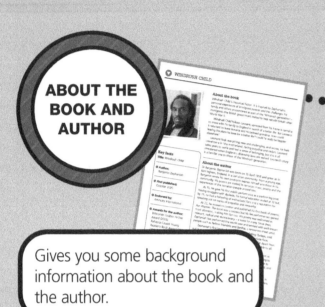

ABOUT THE BOOK AND AUTHOR

Gives you some background information about the book and the author.

GUIDED READING

Breaks the book down into sections and gives notes for using it, ideal for use with the whole class. A bookmark has been provided on page 12 containing **comprehension** questions. The children can be directed to refer to these as they read. Find comprehensive guided reading sessions on the supporting online resources.

SHARED READING

Provides extracts from the children's book with associated notes for focused work. There is also one non-fiction extract that relates to the children's book.

GRAMMAR, PUNCTUATION & SPELLING

Provides word-level work related to the children's book so you can teach grammar, punctuation, spelling and **vocabulary** in context.

PLOT, CHARACTER & SETTING

Contains activity ideas focused on the plot, characters and the setting of the story.

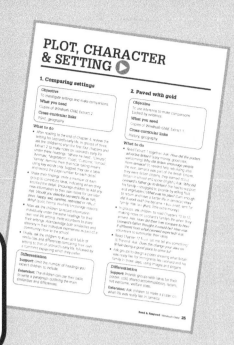

TALK ABOUT IT

Oracy, **fluency**, and speaking and listening activities. These activities may be based directly on the children's book or be broadly based on the themes and concepts of the story.

Provides writing activities related to the children's book. These activities may be based directly on the children's book or be broadly based on the themes and concepts of the story.

GET WRITING

ASSESSMENT

Contains short activities that will help you assess whether the children have understood concepts and curriculum objectives. They are designed to be informal activities to feed into your planning.

Online you can find a host of supporting documents including planning information, comprehensive guided reading sessions and guidance on teaching reading.

www.scholastic.co.uk/read-and-respond/books/windrush-child/online-resources
Access key: Return

SUPPORTING ONLINE RESOURCE

Help children develop a love of reading for pleasure.

Activities

The activities follow the same format:

- **Objective:** the objective for the lesson. It will be based upon a curriculum objective, but will often be more specific to the focus being covered.

- **What you need:** a list of resources you need to teach the lesson, including photocopiable pages.

- **What to do:** the activity notes.

- **Differentiation:** this is provided where specific and useful differentiation advice can be given to support and/or extend the learning in the activity. Differentiation by providing additional adult support has not been included as this will be at a teacher's discretion based upon specific children's needs and ability, as well as the availability of support.

The activities are numbered for reference within each section and should move through the text sequentially – so you can use the lesson while you are reading the book. Once you have read the book, most of the activities can be used in any order you wish.

Section	Activity	Curriculum objectives
Guided reading		Comprehension: To maintain positive attitudes to reading and understanding of what they read.
Shared reading	1	Comprehension: To discuss and evaluate how authors use language, including figurative language, considering the impact on the reader.
	2	Comprehension: To draw inferences such as inferring characters' feelings, thoughts and motives from their actions, and justifying inferences with evidence; identifying how language, structure and presentation contribute to meaning.
	3	Comprehension: To identify how language, structure and presentation contribute to meaning.
	4	Comprehension: To summarise the main ideas drawn from more than one paragraph, identifying key details that support the main ideas.
Grammar, punctuation & spelling	1	Composition: To recognise vocabulary and structures that are appropriate for formal speech and writing, including subjunctive forms.
	2	Composition: To use modal verbs or adverbs to indicate degrees of possibility.
	3	Transcription: To spell some words with 'silent' letters (for example, knight, psalm, solemn).
	4	Composition: To indicate grammatical and other features by using semicolons, colons or dashes to mark boundaries between independent clauses.
	5	Comprehension: To explore the meaning of words in context.
	6	Composition: To use expanded noun phrases to convey complicated information concisely.
Plot, character & setting	1	Comprehension: To maintain positive attitudes to reading and understanding of what they read by making comparisons within and across books. Composition: To consider how authors have developed settings.
	2	Comprehension: To understand what they read by drawing inferences such as inferring characters' feelings, thoughts and motives from their actions, and justifying inferences with evidence.
	3	Comprehension: To understand what they read by drawing inferences such as inferring characters' feelings, thoughts and motives from their actions, and justifying inferences with evidence.
	4	Comprehension: To read books that are structured in different ways.
	5	Comprehension: To understand what they read by summarising the main ideas drawn from more than one paragraph, identifying key details that support the main ideas; to draw inferences such as inferring characters' feelings, thoughts and motives from their actions, and justifying inferences with evidence.
	6	Comprehension: To maintain positive attitudes to reading and understanding of what they read by making comparisons within and across books; to identify how language, structure and presentation contribute to meaning.
	7	Comprehension: To read books that are structured in different ways; to identify how language, structure and presentation contribute to meaning.
	8	Comprehension: To identify and discuss themes and conventions in and across a wide range of writing.

Section	Activity	Curriculum objectives
Talk about it	1	Spoken language: To participate in performances and role play.
	2	Spoken language: To participate in discussions.
	3	Spoken language: To speak audibly and fluently with an increasing command of Standard English; to participate in presentations.
	4	Spoken language: To ask relevant questions to extend their understanding and knowledge; use relevant strategies to build their vocabulary.
	5	Spoken language: To participate in role play.
	6	Spoken language: To articulate and justify answers, arguments and opinions.
Get writing	1	Composition: To draft and write by using further organisational and presentational devices to structure text and to guide the reader (for example, headings, bullet points, underlining).
	2	Composition: To plan their writing by identifying the audience for and purpose of the writing.
	3	Composition: To draft and write by, in narratives, describing settings, characters and atmosphere and integrating dialogue to convey character and advance the action.
	4	Composition: To plan their writing by, in writing narratives, considering how authors have developed characters and settings in what pupils have read. To write by, in narratives, describing settings, characters and atmosphere.
	5	Composition: To plan their writing by identifying the audience for and purpose of the writing, selecting the appropriate form.
	6	Composition: To draft and write by précising longer passages.
Assessment	1	Spoken language: To listen and respond appropriately to adults and their peers. Comprehension: To summarise the main ideas drawn from more than one paragraph, identifying key details that support the main ideas.
	2	Composition: To distinguish between the language of speech and writing and choose the appropriate register.
	3	Composition: To draft and write by using a wide range of devices to build cohesion within and across paragraphs.
	4	Spoken language: To participate in presentations.
	5	Transcription: To use dictionaries to check the spelling and meaning of words; use knowledge of morphology and etymology in spelling and understand that the spelling of some words needs to be learnt specifically.
	6	Comprehension: To understand what they read by checking that the book makes sense to them, discussing their understanding and exploring the meaning of words in context.

Key facts

Title: *Windrush Child*

⦿ **Author:**
Benjamin Zephaniah

⦿ **First published:**
October 2020

⦿ **Endorsed by:**
Amnesty International

⦿ **Awards for the author:**
Wisconsin Golden Archer
Award (2003)
Rebecca Caudill Young
Reader's Book Award (2004)
Utah Beehive Award (2004)
California Young Reader
Medal (2005)
Iowa Teen Award (2005)
South Carolina Junior Book
Award (2005)

About the book

Windrush Child is historical fiction. It is inspired by Zephaniah's personal experience of immigrant parents and the challenges his family and others encountered as part of the 'Windrush generation'– immigrants the British government invited to help rebuild Britain after World War II.

Windrush Child follows Leonard, uprooted from his home in Jamaica to move with his family to England in search of a better life. But Leonard is reluctant to leave Jamaica and his beloved grandma. How could leaving the place he loves be 'a better life'? Could he really be happier elsewhere?

Leonard finds everything new and challenging, and worse, he feels unwelcome in 'the motherland', facing prejudice and racism. Leonard takes years to settle and feel a sense of belonging, but this is all threatened when England's citizenship laws are revised. Leonard's story is a familiar one to those of the Windrush generation.

About the author

Dr Benjamin Zephaniah was born on 15 April 1958 and grew up in Birmingham, England, in a Jamaican community. From a young age, Benjamin wrote his own poetry to express himself and those in his community. His poems are rooted in Jamaican music, poetry and the experiences of the Jamaican people around him.

At 10, he gave his first public performance as a performing poet. Having struggled with dyslexia, his formal education ended at 13 but, by 15, he had a following of enthusiastic fans and a reputation for speaking out on topics of prejudice and inequality.

At 22, he moved to London and published his first book of poems, *Pen Rhythm*. The book was a success but his live performances gained most attention, making him famous. His poetry was welcomed as relevant, radical and revolutionary – a voice for many. Since then, Zephaniah has performed the world over and worked with well-known people such as Nelson Mandela and Banksy, a renowned street artist.

Zephaniah's first book of children's poetry, *Talking Turkeys*, sold out in six weeks. His bestselling young adult novels include *Face, Gangsta Rap, Teacher's Dead, Refugee Boy* and *Terror Kid*. Apart from highlighting issues, Zephaniah aims to make reading accessible to all. About his latest book, *Windrush Child*, he says:

'I am a Windrush Child. It was only by chance that I was born in England. Just a quick decision by my mother… I grew up listening to stories of people of my generation talking about what it was like to grow up in the "mother country". … It was good, but it was bad, and sometimes it was ugly. I like my fiction to be true.'

Zephaniah holds 16 honorary doctorates, has been Writer in Residence at the Africa Arts Collective in Liverpool, Creative Artist in Residence at Cambridge University and was made a Doctor of Letters by the University of Central England (1999).

GUIDED READING ▶

Before reading

Discuss the book title with the children and explain that it relates to real events that still affect people in Britain today. *Empire Windrush* was the name of one of the ships that brought people and their families to live and work in Britain who had been born in countries that used to be part of the British Empire, such as Jamaica. So at the time these people were British citizens. Later on, not only did parts of the Empire became independent countries but Britain's laws also changed, sometimes depriving people from those countries of their right to live and work in Britain as British citizens. This affected many people who had made their homes in Britain for most of their lives and for many it was not their fault that they did not have the documentation later required to stay in Britain legally. Many of these people were made to feel unwelcome and suffered racist abuse.

Exploring (Prologue and Chapter 1)

Invite the children to explore the book's cover, back and front. Ask: *What clues indicate the book's genre?* (The review and description of the 'Voices' series indicate historical fiction.) Ask: *What are this genre's features?* (It is set in past with mostly fictitious characters but authentic detail.) The story spans 1947–2018; discuss that even yesterday counts as history. Ask: *What else does the cover suggest about the plot?* (It is about Leonard, a young, black boy who moves from Jamaica to England, and his experiences.) Turn to the prologue and together discuss question 14 on the bookmark. Read the prologue with the children. Ask: *What can you tell about the person in the prologue?* (An old man with African ancestry, he is alone, unhappy and feels it's unjust that he's there.) Ask: *What is the point of a prologue?* (It adds interest to a story by focusing on an earlier time, highlighting a later event to create suspense, looking back on the story events or more generally foreshadowing later events.) The children may find this introduction difficult; don't dwell on it as it will make more sense at the end.

Before reading Chapter 1, locate Jamaica on a map and find out what the children know about it. After reading, ask: *Who discovered Jamaica?* (This is unknown but the Taíno and Arawak were there before Christopher Columbus arrived.) Ask: *Why do people in Jamaica speak English?* Briefly review Jamaica's history as set out in the chapter, why England fought Spain and why the slave trade meant many people from Africa (and other places) came to Jamaica.

Maroon town (Chapters 2 to 5)

Ask the children to read Chapters 2 and 3 independently. Ask the children to describe Leonard's life in Jamaica (such as: fun, carefree, good weather, safe, mother is a domestic worker, dad went to England when Leonard was a baby, lives with Grandma, poor but happy, hurricanes). Ask the children to discuss question 1 on the bookmark in groups. Invite a spokesperson to summarise each group's views. ('God Save the Queen' and 'Rule Britannia' show England governed Jamaica; English versions of history were taught in schools; Britain invited Jamaicans to come to England; being welcomed as British citizens; Leonard's dad believing he would have opportunities to build a better life.) Read Chapter 4 to the children. Ask: *Why was Leonard's grandma upset?* (She was missing Leonard's grandpa and knew Leonard and his mum were moving to England.) Ask: *Why is Leonard so upset?* (He loves his home and grandma; was always told his dad would come back; felt lied to.) Ask the children to read Chapter 5 independently, considering question 2 on the bookmark, then share ideas, asking for evidence to support them.

Shipboard (Chapters 6 to 8)

After the children read Chapters 6 to 8, ask: *Why didn't Leonard have a passport?* (He was too young.) Leonard being undocumented is a clue to what happens at the end of the book and the prologue.

Link to your earlier discussion about *Windrush* and explain that this man is in detention. Ask: *Why might he feel upset about being there?* (Possibly one of the people being deprived of the right to live in Britain; don't explain too much – just enough to provide context for the story.) A critical aspect of the Windrush scandal that erupted 50 years later was that many who arrived as part of the Windrush generation had no documentation to prove they had arrived legally in Britain and so were vulnerable to later policy changes on immigration and the right to live in Britain. Ask: *Whom did Leonard befriend on board the ship?* (Winston) Build a mind map to collate everything the children know about Winston. Ask: *Was Winston black or white?* (unclear) Encourage the children to notice that Leonard's descriptions of most people on board do not include colour – it is not yet relevant to him. It is worth noting Winston, as he reappears later on.

Arrival (Chapters 9 to 12)

Ask: *Have you ever been anywhere new – a place that is completely different to what you already know? Or moved from a different country? Have you experienced not fitting in and being made to feel unwelcome?* After discussing their experiences, ask the children to read Chapters 9 and 10 independently. Ask: *What was difficult about arriving in England for Leonard?* (The cold, smells, not saying goodbye to Winston, scenery, greyness, silence, meeting his dad.) Ask: *Why was Leonard rude to his dad?* (He was scared, lonely, missing home and Grandma.) Read Chapters 11 and 12 together. Ask: *How was life different from Jamaica for Leonard?* (It was cold, there was a lack of freedom, being stared at, different food, few and different animals, lack of respect for elders.) Ask: *Why does Leonard's relationship with his dad improve?* (playing football, talking about life, shared experiences) Together discuss question 3 on the bookmark. Sensitively, explain the terminology in use at the time – 'coloured' as opposed to 'black' – and why some places were only for white people. Use his dad's explanation as a guide. Ask: *Did his dad's explanation help Leonard understand why they were sometimes treated badly? Did it make things better?* Encourage the children to empathise with Leonard.

Settling in (Chapters 13 to 17)

Bearing in mind questions 3, 4 and 11 on the bookmark, ask the children to read Chapters 13 to 16. Share ideas. Ask: *Why did Leonard find it hard to make friends?* (Nobody else was from Jamaica or black, he had a different accent, there were stereotypical ideas about black people, ignorance and prejudice.) Ask: *Why did Leonard's mum say there was 'a time to speak and a time to stay silent'?* (They were outsiders, it was not their country although they were British, they didn't want to cause trouble.) *How was this different from what Grandma taught him?* (Grandma taught Leonard to always say how he felt.) At the end of Chapter 16, ask: *Why did Leonard stop speaking to Mark?* (Mark showed ignorance about Leonard and Jamaica, like everyone else.) Use the children's answers to discuss question 12 on the bookmark.

Read Chapter 17 together and begin to discuss question 13 on the bookmark. Talk about first-person narrative and how the reader sees things from the narrator's perspective – at this stage, that of a 10-year-old boy far from home with limited understanding of the social and political tensions in his new environment. Slowly, the children follow Leonard's journey as he grows accustomed to his new life and all it entails, both good and bad. Keep a wall chart, listing good and bad aspects of life in Manchester for Leonard and his family.

Trouble (Chapters 18 to 25)

At the end of Chapter 19, ask: *What made it harder for Leonard to be positive?* (His dad was beaten up.) Together, begin discussing question 5 on the bookmark. Ask: *Why does Leonard feel his life isn't better?* (He was bullied, Mum put down, Dad beaten up, he can do nothing about it.) Read Chapters 20 to 25 together and discuss the events sensitively. Historically, although family units tended to be bounded by marriage, long periods of separation made life lonely and challenging. Loyalty is a strong theme in the book. Despite his lapse, Leonard's father was loyal to his family, always providing for them and seeking to create a better life.

Together, begin discussing question 15 on the bookmark. Encourage the children to notice how challenging life was for Leonard's parents. Ask: *Why did they stay in England when they faced so* many hardships? (They were determined to create a better life for Leonard; the welfare state provided many things free; life wasn't easy in Jamaica – different challenges, such as poverty, hurricanes and limited opportunities.) Ask: *What important event occurred in 1962?* (Jamaican independence) Ask: *If independence had happened earlier, do you think Leonard's dad would have gone to England?* (It would have been harder as they wouldn't have been British citizens.)

Moving on (Chapters 26 to 31)

It seems as if life is working out well for Leonard and his family, yet his mum still feels Jamaica's call. Ask: *Is Jamaica still home for Leonard?* (no) Ask the children to think about questions 6 and 8 on the bookmark as they read Chapter 31. The timeline moves quickly from Leonard's life at 16 to events in the final chapter when he is 71. Note important events, for example, Leonard's first job, his first girlfriend, getting beaten up, his dad dying, getting married, his mum returning to Jamaica, having a child, watching the world change, his mother getting ill, contact with family in Jamaica, retiring, deciding to visit his mum in Maroon Town. Thinking about the organisation of the book, at the end of Chapter 31, ask children to predict whether the trip will go smoothly. The final sentence implies it will not.

Structure and themes (Chapter 32)

Before reading the final chapter, ask the children to consider question 16 on the bookmark. Discuss whether his dad's original aim of creating a better life was achieved; note points for and against on the board. Ask: *Did Britain greet Jamaicans with the 'hand of friendship'? Were they welcomed as the posters in Chapter 2 suggested? If not, why not?* (Maybe at first they were needed and welcomed, but not everyone wanted Jamaicans or other immigrants. Over time, attitudes and social conditions changed – some for the better and some not.) Discuss question 7 on the bookmark, inviting suggestions backed by evidence: friendship (Winston, Mark, Michael and Rosie Barry, Anna, Fred, Marie), loyalty (to culture, family, Britain, Jamaica), identity (being black, Jamaican, British, a person with feelings), racism (alienation, stereotyping, name-calling,

prejudice, ignorance) and betrayal (Shirley, reality of life in Britain compared to promises, Britain's final treatment of Leonard).

Read Chapter 32 with the children and discuss question 9 on the bookmark. The final chapter makes sense of the prologue. Discuss why Leonard was detained. Ask: *What clues foreshadowed the ending earlier in the book?* (Leonard had no passport – no record of arriving legally in Britain; Winston had a wealthy family.) Ask: *Why did Winston's life differ from Leonard's?* (He had a passport, a good education, became a lawyer – wealth protected him and provided opportunities.) Ask the children to think about question 18 on the bookmark. Point out that the final chapter occurs in 2018 – yet it is still history. Talk about how what happens in the past can affect the present. Ask the children to re-read the first three sentences of Chapter 1. Ask: *How is Leonard 'history'?* Leonard's story represents the experiences of many, making it an important part of black history as well as English and world history. Britain's colonial past explains why English history dominated the Jamaican school system. His family taught Leonard his Jamaican history and culture at home via the oral tradition and ways of life; Fred, his apprentice master, taught him that history is made by everyday people, not just by kings, queens, armies and prominent people. Ask: *Do you think historical fiction is a good way to learn about history? Why?* Discuss other historical fiction they have read and what they learned.

Discuss question 10 on the bookmark. The story has many pivotal moments along a timeline of a person's life, similar to an autobiography. Although it is fiction, it doesn't follow a standard story structure. The story has no resolution and conclusion. Discuss question 17 on the bookmark. Ask: *Does the end satisfy you?* Leonard's story, representing the story of many real people like him, is still unfolding. Ask: *Do you think it's important that the author believes he is part of the Windrush generation?* (adds authenticity) Finally, revisit question 16 on the bookmark and ask the children if their views have changed after reading the final chapter.

Windrush Child
By Benjamin Zephaniah

Focus on... Meaning

1. Why does the Queen of England matter to Leonard and his family in Jamaica?

2. Predict whether Leonard will enjoy being in England when he first gets there.

3. What makes people in England regard Leonard as different?

4. Why do some people in England treat Leonard and his family badly?

5. Why does Leonard's mother return to Jamaica after living so long in England?

6. Does Leonard have a 'better life' in England?

7. What themes are developed during the novel?

Focus on... Organisation

8. Why is more time spent describing Leonard's early life than his later life?

9. How does the end of the book link back to its beginning?

10. How does the book's organisation differ from standard story structure: introduction, build-up, complication or challenge, climax, resolution and conclusion?

Windrush Child
By Benjamin Zephaniah

Focus on... Language and features

11. What is the effect of seeing events through Leonard's eyes?

12. What makes the names Leonard is called unkind or unfair?

13. How does the dialogue reflect where people come from?

Focus on... Purpose, viewpoints and effects

14. What is the purpose of a prologue?

15. How would the story be different if it were told from Leonard's mum's or dad's perspective?

16. Do you think Leonard's dad would have chosen to go to England if he had known what would happen to his family?

17. What is the effect of not knowing what happens to Leonard?

18. Why is this novel called historical fiction?

SHARED READING ▶

Extract 1

- Hand out enlarged copies of the extract and have the children follow as you read, modelling fluency and expression. Encourage them to notice your reading techniques; for example, emphasis and pauses.

- Draw a table on the board. Ask: *What made Leonard's mum and dad happy or unhappy?* (Mum unhappy: early life, no family contact, trials and tribulations; happy: meeting Leonard's dad, Leonard's birth. Dad happy: meeting mother and Leonard's birth; unhappy: not being able to provide for his family.) Discuss how their feelings of happiness went up and down compared to each other.

- Re-read the extract together using choral reading with the children focusing on fluency and expression. Ask: *Why did Leonard's dad go to Britain?* (To help Britain rebuild and earn money – Britain was advertising opportunities.) Ask: *What does the 'mum country' mean?* (As Jamaica was part of British Empire, Britain was referred to as the 'mum country'.)

- Now ask the children to re-read independently, focusing on figurative language. Ask: *What does it mean to have 'a cloud hanging over' you? Is it literal or figurative language?* (It means something is upsetting/worrying you; figurative.) Ask the children to underline three examples of figurative language in the second paragraph and explain what they mean. ('land of opportunity': place with many opportunities to do well; 'streets would be paved with gold': easy place to earn lots of money; the 'great British hand of friendship': Britain would welcome them as friends and look after them.)

- Finally, ask: *How do you think Leonard's father felt when he wrote the postcard? Why?* (Optimistic, proud, confident; he believes the posters – that he will do well for himself and his family.)

Extract 2

- Provide enlarged copies of the extract for the children to read independently, focusing on the contrast between Jamaica and Manchester. Invite volunteers to summarise the differences and log their responses on a mind map (temperature, manner of walking, scenery, lack of freedom, animals, greeting elders). Ask: *How is Leonard feeling?* (He is feeling restricted, homesick, strange, different.) Ask: *Why do you think Leonard wanted to 'roar'? Why didn't he?* (He wanted to express his feelings but didn't want to upset his parents more.)

- Ask the children to locate and circle two examples of a semicolon. Ask: *Why is a semicolon used?* (To mark the boundary between independent clauses; the clauses are closely related enough to belong in one sentence, despite being independent.)

- Ask the children to discuss different uses of the comma in groups. After discussion, go through the extract and invite volunteers to explain whether the commas set off an adverbial, separate clauses, introduce dialogue or separate list items to ensure clarity of meaning. Then demonstrate how commas help indicate pauses for reading aloud and listen to volunteers reading the different paragraphs.

- Finally, discuss the theme of identity. Ask: *Why does Leonard prefer to stay indoors? What does this tell you about how he feels?* (So white people can't stare at them; feels different: his background, how he acts, his colour.) Ask: *What might make Leonard feel more at home?* (For example, a friend.) Encourage the children to empathise by thinking of a time when they have felt isolated or different. Ask: *What helped you?*

Extract 3

- Arrange the children in groups of three. Provide copies of the extract and ask them to prepare and practise a dramatic reading: narrator and two voices for the dialogue. Explain that groups of volunteers will read to the class, who will give feedback, guided by you, on what they did well relating to punctuation, pace, fluency, intonation and expression.

- Explain the historical context of the colour bar. Leonard's dad later explains how much worse it was for black people in America at that time. Ask: *Why did the shopkeeper put up the notice?* (Many people were ignorant and prejudiced against people who looked or sounded different, or who had historically been slaves; many were reluctant to engage with them and shopkeepers feared people wouldn't come into their shops if they served them.) Ask: *How do you think Leonard and his dad feel in the extract?* (Leonard: puzzled; Dad: frustrated, resigned, even angry.) Discuss how life has changed since Leonard arrived in England.

- Ask: *Who is the narrator? How can you tell?* (Leonard: 'I', 'my', 'me' pronouns in narrative.) Ask: *What is the effect of Leonard as the narrator?* (The story is from his point of view; readers share his feelings, reactions and understanding.) Invite the children to discuss other first-person narrative books they have read and explain whether they enjoy the style.

- Ask: *Why is this book called historical fiction?* (It is set in the past, has authentic historical detail: setting, events, lives, and so on.) Invite the children to find examples in the extract. Ask: *What other genre of writing is it similar to? Why?* (Autobiography: someone recounts the events of their life even though fictional.)

Extract 4

- Hand out enlarged copies of Extract 4. In pairs, invite the children to skim and identify the type, purpose and features of the text. (Non-fiction, giving historical and geographical background, organised into sections with headings, lists with bullets, diagram, picture and questions with answers, layout is visually effective, appealing and easy to read.)

- Explore the difference between a fact (something that can be proved) and an opinion (personal belief or view, not based on proof). Suggest the children use different-coloured markers to highlight, A: facts about the ship; B: facts about the people on the ship. Ask: *Are there any opinions in this text?* (no) Ask: *Why?* (Non-fiction, factual text aimed to inform and provide objective information about a historical event.)

- Explain the meaning of topic-specific words such as 'long tons' (imperial not metric ton – 1016.047kg or 2240lb), 'deadweight' (literally, the ship's load including the weight of cargo and passengers; or figuratively, something or someone that is a burden), and 'tonnage' (the size and capacity of a ship or the weight of the cargo in tons).

- Explore focus words from the text such as: 'generation', 'culture', 'citizens', 'destination', 'contribution'. Use the 'Focus word table' from the supporting online resources (see page 5) to provide everyday explanations, find dictionary definitions, and then encourage children to use the words in different contexts by writing sentences.

- In pairs, ask children to create a mind map to summarise the text. To assist, draw a skeleton mind map on the board with the main topic surrounded by four sub-topics. They complete the mind map using key words and phrases under each sub-topic. They can use it to write a summary paragraph.

- Have a class quiz as a plenary to check their understanding of the text.

Extract 1

Grandma was always talking to me, but Mum never talked much about her life. She just told me she didn't have any contact with her family, and she had a life of suffering. A life of trials and tribulations. She told me that meeting my dad brought her great happiness, and my birth brought her more happiness. She told me that dad was also happy of course, but he was only happy for a while. Then it was as if there was a cloud hanging over him. He felt that he could not continue to feed his family by selling vegetables and doing odd jobs. He felt that the family were poor because of him.

The British government had posters all over Jamaica telling people that they would be welcome to come to Britain, to help rebuild the country because the war had left it in ruins. Jamaicans were told on radio and in town halls that Britain was the 'land of opportunity' where 'the streets would soon be paved with gold'. They were told that they would be greeted with the great British hand of friendship, because they were British citizens, and they were welcomed in the mum country. My dad couldn't resist. He felt that he had to do something, for Britain and for himself, so seven months after I was born, he boarded a ship and sailed to England. He promised mum that after a few years of work he would return, and everything would be all right.

So my dad left when I was just a baby. As soon as he landed, he sent a letter back to Mum and Grandma, and a postcard for me. The postcard had a picture of the ship that took him to England. It was called the *Empire Windrush*. On the back of the card he wrote,

I am a Windrush man,
so you, my child,
are a Windrush Child.

Extract 2

I began to understand why people walked so fast in England. It was to keep warm. Copying them, I began to walk fast when I was cold, and it worked! Well, it helped. If I walked fast in Jamaica, I would get too hot and tired, but in Manchester it made sense. The city was noisy and busy. There were pubs on many of the street corners, factories with smoke coming from their chimneys, and large cinemas, but the tallest buildings of all were the churches. Down the side streets children played on the road, and dogs roamed freely. I began getting used to it but it felt nothing like the freedom of sprinting through the trees of Maroon Town, or running around the palm trees only to come home and tumble into my grandma's embrace. I couldn't complain. I didn't want to upset my parents any more, so I kept my feelings to myself. I thought of my grandma's words; 'Lions always roar.' I wanted to roar louder than ever before.

Everywhere that I went, Mum or Dad were always with me; I couldn't go out and play freely like I used to. I saw cats and dogs in Manchester, but I missed the goats, the lizards, the mongooses, and the hummingbirds of Jamaica. I missed all the wild animals I used to chase when they were not chasing me. After a while I got used to staying indoors and began to prefer it because the white people couldn't stare at us there.

It was strange to see young people and children just walking past elders and not saying good morning or good evening. In Jamaica, in the area where I lived, we kids always had to say hello to the elders. If we didn't, the message would reach home, sometimes before we got there ourselves. If I forgot, the elder I'd ignored would tell my mum, 'Your son pass me this morning and never bother say hello.' Then when I got home there would be trouble.

Extract 3

As we walked back home, on a corner of the high street I spotted a shop selling food and drinks. It was a small, colourful shop, and one window displayed lots of sweets and cakes. I stopped Dad and nodded towards the shop. Dad just shook his head.

'Sorry, son. We can't go in there.'

'Why not? Those cakes look nice, and they have soft fruit drinks.'

'They have a colour bar there,' Dad said still shaking his head.

'What's a colour bar?' I asked.

My dad used his arm that was still around my shoulder and guided me closer to the door. With his other hand he pointed to a hand-written notice on the door:

SORRY. WE DON'T SERVE COLOUREDS HERE.

'What are coloureds?' I asked.

'That's what they call us,' he replied. 'They call us coloured because of our skin.'

'So we can't go in?'

'No. Don't worry about that. There are other places.'

We walked for less than a minute when we came to another shop selling drinks where we entered and bought a cake each and some fruit juice in glass bottles. We began to eat as we walked, then we walked into a church yard and sat down on a bench.

'If we call ourselves black people, why do they call us coloured?' I asked, still puzzled by the sign.

'There are some white people who think that white is de best, de standard, and everyone else is coloured. And because they think they are the best, they think they have de right to rule over us. You know 'bout slavery?'

'Yes,' I replied.

'Well, some people still think like they did back then. They can't keep us in slavery any more, but they still want to control us.'

'But can they do that?' I asked.

'Put it like this, son, there's no law stopping them.'

Extract 4

The Windrush generation

The Windrush generation are immigrants who arrived in England on a ship called HMT *Empire Windrush* between 1948 and 1973. They came from Caribbean countries such as Jamaica, Trinidad and Tobago, and Barbados.

SHIP FACT FILE

Length: 500ft 3in (152.48m)
Beam: 65ft 7in (19.99m)
Depth: 37ft 8in (11.48m)
Propulsion: 4 diesel engines driving two propellers
Speed: 14.5 knots (26.9km/h)
Tonnage: 8530 long tons deadweight

HMT *Empire Windrush*

THE FIRST PEOPLE TO ARRIVE ON THE WINDRUSH

Who?	When?	Where?	How long?	How much did it cost?	What were their jobs and skills?
• 1027 passengers • More than half from Jamaica • More men than women • 86 children of 12 years and under	Arrived on the morning of 21 June 1948	Docked at the port of Tilbury, Essex, near London	30 days	£28 (about £1000 today)	mechanic, judge, nurse, carpenter, tailor, welder, engineer, shoemaker, hairdresser, electrician, piano repairer, potter, boxer, student, musician, painter

CHALLENGES – THEN AND NOW

Coming from a warm climate, the immigrants faced cold weather, strange food, a different culture and even racism. After living and working in Britain for many years, they had new problems when England changed its immigration rules. Many had no record of arriving in England, as children often did not have passports when they arrived. Some are still fighting for the right to live and work in Britain as British citizens.

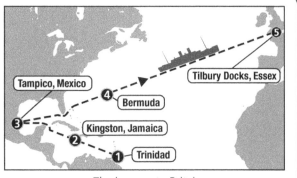

The journey to Britain

DID YOU KNOW?

London was the most popular destination for the Caribbean passengers.
'Windrush Day' is now celebrated in Britain to acknowledge the Caribbean community and their contribution to British society.

GRAMMAR, PUNCTUATION & SPELLING ▶

1. Formal and informal

Objective
To identify differences in vocabulary and structure typical of informal and formal speech.

What you need
Copies of *Windrush Child.*

What to do
- Discuss the main differences between dialogue and narrative to ascertain what the children already know (tenses, formality/register, flexible grammar, contractions, use of slang and colloquial expressions, and so on).

- Read the first two pages of Chapter 9. At the end of the first paragraph, ask: *What's informal about Mum's question?* (Statement but with question mark; no inversion.) Ask: *How does Leonard know it's a question?* (Context; voice goes up at end.)

- Invite a volunteer to explain what is informal about what Mum says next (omits 'It' at beginning; short sentence with no verb; dialect term ('ting'); question not structured as one). Ask: *Is the man in uniform's question formal or informal? Why?* (Formal words and structure; use of the word 'madam'.)

- Ask the children to note further informal speech examples (contraction: 'can't'; 'de' not 'the'; 'she does kindness' – colloquial). Ask: *What's the difference between an accent and a dialect?* (Accent: different pronunciation; dialect: involves different words and grammar.) Ask: *Can you tell if someone has an accent in a book?* (Only by inferring from speech patterns and vocabulary.)

Differentiation
Support: Ask the children to rephrase the two questions as they would normally ask them. Discuss their answers in small groups, pointing out the inversion or other question words.

Extension: Tell children to log further dialect examples (grammar and vocabulary) in Leonard's family's speech patterns that reveal their Jamaican heritage.

2. Likely, possible or unlikely?

Objective
To indicate possibility using modals.

What you need
Copies of *Windrush Child.*

What to do
- Revise auxiliary (helping) verbs. Ask: *Which verbs act as auxiliary verbs to form verb tenses?* ('be' and 'have') Give some examples of sentences that contain auxiliary verbs: *He is walking to school, She has driven to work, Sarah was going to town.* Ask the class to identify the tense, the main verb and auxiliary verb in each. Ask for other examples.

- Write the following modal verbs on the board: 'would', 'should', 'can', 'could', 'must', 'might', 'may', 'will' and recap as necessary. Then read Chapter 14 from 'Dad bought a small black-and-white television…' to '…I learned a lot more', noting modals ('would', 'should'). Look at each example of 'would' and discuss the possibility: likely/definitely, possible, unlikely. Ask: *How do they change if you replace 'would' with 'could', 'might' or 'wouldn't'?* (could/might: possible rather than likely; wouldn't: unlikely)

- If time permits, discuss that modals can also express permission (may, can), ability (can, could) and obligation/advice (must, should). Ask: *In the Chapter 14 extract, did 'should' express ability, permission or obligation?* (obligation) Invite volunteers to invent sentences using the modals listed on the board and discuss what they express. For example, Leonard often says 'could' and 'couldn't' expressing ability: 'I couldn't believe…'

Differentiation
Support: Discuss further sentences containing modals with small groups to practise identifying what they express.

Extension: Ask children to scan for modals as they read on, noting what they express.

3. Silent but important

Objective
To spell words with 'silent' letters.

What you need
Copies of *Windrush Child*, dictionaries, photocopiable page 22 'Silent but important'.

What to do

- Divide the board into three columns headed: 'beginning', 'middle', 'end'. Then write an example word with a silent letter under each, underlining the silent letter (write, foreign, lamb). Invite volunteers to suggest other silent letter words writing them on the board, until you have identified the common silent letters: 'b', 'c', 'g', 'h', 'k', 'l', 'n', 'p', 't', 'u', 'w'. Discuss the usual position of the silent letter – some can appear in different places ('gnaw', 'foreign', 'wrong', 'answer').

- Explain that many English words come from languages such as French, Latin, Greek, German and Old English, which over time have introduced silent letters into English spelling. Ask the children to complete photocopiable page 22 'Silent but important' as practice. (Answers: 1. plumber, 2. school, 3. lamb, 4. pneumonia, 5. wrong, 6. doubt, 7. hour, 8. island, 9. know, 10. listen, 11. foreigner, 12. sword)

- Next, ask pairs to choose one or two silent letters and find words containing them in *Windrush Child*. They should write each word on a slip of paper with the silent letter in a different colour. Encourage children to use dictionaries. Then bring the class together and create a silent letter display, organised by letter or position in the word.

Differentiation

Support: Children can use dictionaries instead of *Windrush Child*. Allocate pairs silent letters at the beginning of words.

Extension: Ask pairs of children to suggest a silent letter for their partner. Their partner should volunteer words with that silent letter.

4. Dash

Objective
To identify how dashes are used.

What you need
Copies of *Windrush Child*, photocopiable page 23 'Dash'.

What to do

- Revise hyphens. Ask: *What is a hyphen and what is its purpose?* (A short line with no space either side, creates compound words, avoids ambiguity.) Use the chapter headings from Chapter 21 onwards to demonstrate. Invite volunteers to give other examples (from the book where possible): 'black-eyed peas', 'long-distance running', 'fold-down bed', 'black-and-white television'.

- Revise dashes (longer lines, space either side, single or in pairs). Ask: *What are the functions of a dash?* (In pairs, as brackets/parenthesis; singly, to add an afterthought or additional information – also a form of parenthesis but no text after the additional detail or afterthought.) Ask: *What punctuation can be used instead of dashes to indicate parenthesis?* (Brackets or commas but dashes are more informal.) Turn to Chapter 16 and ask: *How are dashes used in this chapter?* (To add an afterthought – or additional information.) Ask: *Why do you think dashes are often used in this novel?* They fit the book's first-person narrative style, echoing how Leonard thinks as he recounts his story – adding an afterthought or further explanation as one might do when speaking or remembering.

- Ask the children to complete photocopiable page 23 'Dash' independently.

Differentiation

Support: Underline the additional information in the sentences to help children identify where the dashes go.

Extension: Ask the children to invent sentences for a partner to add appropriate dashes – sometimes one and sometimes two.

5. Words in context

Objective

To discuss and explore the meaning of words in context.

What you need

Copies of *Windrush Child*, 'Focus word table' from the supporting online resource (see page 5).

What to do

- Hand out copies of the 'Focus word table'. Explain you will use it to explore words from the text.

- Read the penultimate paragraph of Chapter 28. After reading, identify the focus words – 'core', 'attitude', 'sacrificed' – for the children to write in column 1 'Focus word'. Then give the children child-friendly meanings to write in column 2 'Everyday explanation', followed by an example sentence:
  core: middle or centre – I ate the apple down to its core
  attitude: the way you act or think about something – she has a positive attitude to school
  sacrificed: give up something (precious or important) – he sacrificed playing soccer to finish his project.
  Now ask the children to complete the final column, 'Definition', using their dictionaries.

- Return to the words in the text and discuss each in context, with guiding questions. *What does Leonard mean by his core here? What does Leonard's shifting attitude mean? Does he still feel like an outsider or does he now feel British? Would Leonard's dad have felt that what he sacrificed was worth it? What did he want for Leonard?*

- Next, organise the class into small groups to play 'Three Things': Think of three things that have a core. Name three things you have a positive or negative attitude to. Think of three things you or some you know have sacrificed? End by holding a 'three things' plenary.

Differentiation

Support: Allow groups to focus on one or two words only when playing 'Three Things'.

Extension: Invite children to invent new sentences using the focus words.

6. Efficient description

Objective

To use expanded noun phrases.

What you need

Notebooks, photocopiable page 24 'Efficient description'.

What to do

- Revise phrases: groups of words, with no verb, working together as adjectives, adverbs or nouns. Demonstrate how to expand a noun phrase. Write 'boy' in the middle of the board. Ask: *What was Leonard like?* Use their responses to turn 'boy' into an expanded noun phrase. First, invite suggestions for words before the noun, for example: 'A shy, ten-year-old, Jamaican boy'. Encourage interesting words and then ask: *What sort of words were used to expand 'boy'?* (mostly adjectives and determiners) Remind them that commas separate the adjectives and that determiners such as 'a' or 'the' form part of the noun phrase.

- Next, invite suggestions for further descriptors to add after the noun using 'with', for example, 'with little knowledge of Britain'. Underline the whole noun phrase showing how elements either side of the noun expand it.

- Write the following word pattern on the board: 'a/the adjective, adjective, (adjective) noun with adjective, noun'. As a class, build expanded noun phrases completing the sentence: 'Leonard is…boy…' Follow the pattern and discuss how efficiently a noun phrase provides detailed information to bring writing to life. Be flexible about how many adjectives precede the noun and what follows but it must contain no verb. If necessary, practise with other nouns before asking the class to complete photocopiable page 24 'Efficient description' independently.

Differentiation

Support: Provide children with a word bank to help complete the activity.

Extension: Ask the children to write a descriptive paragraph using at least two expanded noun phrases.

Silent but important

- Read the clues and complete the crossword.

- Circle the silent letter in each answer.

Across

2. Place where children go to be educated (6)

3. Baby sheep (4)

5. Not right (5)

7. Unit of time equal to 60 minutes (4)

10. Pay attention to someone or something to hear them (6)

11. Someone from another country (9)

12. Weapon with long, metal blade and handle, used mostly in the past (5)

Down

1. Person who repairs water pipes and leaks (7)

4. Serious illness where your lungs fill with liquid and it is hard to breathe (9)

6. Feeling of not being certain about something (5)

8. Area of land that has water around it (6)

9. Have knowledge or information about something in your mind (4)

Dash

- Rewrite each sentence using one or two dashes to mark off additional information (parenthesis).

1. Leonard loved Jamaica the place where he was born.

_____

2. Hyde Primary School the first school I attended in Manchester was not my happiest experience.

_____

_____

3. Jamaica an island in the Caribbean was granted independence from Britain in 1962.

_____

_____

4. Leonard always remembered his grandma's advice lions always roar.

_____

5. My suit the only one I had was not warm enough.

_____

- Complete each sentence, adding extra detail after the dash.

1. I used to find it difficult to concentrate at school – _____

_____

2. I didn't have my own passport – _____

_____

3. Why did my parents think living in Britain would be better –

_____

4. Our new flat had much more space – _____

_____

5. My dad explained that when you are old, you still get paid in Britain –

_____

_____

Efficient description

- Circle the expanded noun and underline the entire expanded noun phrase in each sentence.

1. Maroon Town was a crowded, exciting town with cows blocking the roads.

2. We stared at the gigantic, shiny, passenger ship with its wide, open deck.

3. I saw a slight, similar-aged boy, with a suit, shirt, tie and cap.

4. The wild, unpredictable hurricane with its deadly power threatened the whole island.

5. Manchester seemed a cold, grey, unwelcoming place with unfamiliar scenery.

- Create expanded noun phrases following this pattern: adjective, adjective, noun with…

1. _____, _____ school with _____.

2. _____, _____ bully with _____.

3. _____, _____ flat with _____.

4. _____, _____ meal with _____.

5. _____, _____ weather with _____.

- Write a sentence to include one of the expanded noun phrases above.

_____

_____

_____

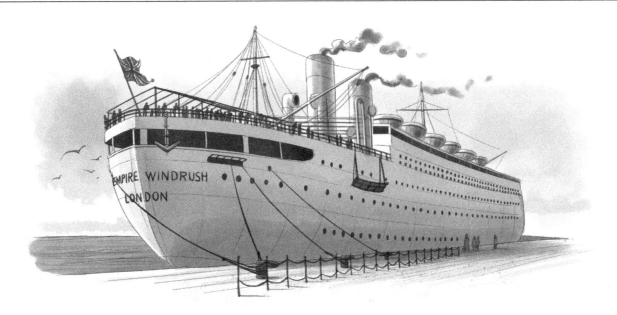

PLOT, CHARACTER & SETTING ▶

1. Comparing settings

> **Objective**
> To investigate settings and make comparisons.
>
> **What you need**
> Copies of *Windrush Child*, Extract 2.
>
> **Cross-curricular links**
> PSHE, geography

What to do

- After reading to the end of Chapter 4, review the setting for Leonard's early life. In groups of three, ask the children to scan the first four chapters and Extract 2 to make notes on Leonard's early life under these headings: 'Where he lived', 'Climate', 'Animals', 'Vegetation', 'Food', 'Customs', 'School', 'Family'. Remind them that note-taking means using key words only. Suggest they use a table and record the page number for each detail.

- Share their findings. Invite a member of each group to contribute ideas, indicating where they sourced the detail. Encourage children to add any new information to their own notes for use later. Ask: *Would you describe Leonard's life as rich, poor, happy, sad, carefree, restricted or other? Why?* (poor, happy, carefree) Encourage reasons.

- Now ask the children to record information individually under the same headings for their own real-life setting. Invite volunteers to share their settings. Acknowledge both similarities and diversity in their individual experiences as part of a community close to the school.

- Finally, ask the children to draw up a table of similarities and differences comparing their own setting to that of Leonard's early life, followed by a comment explaining which they prefer.

> **Differentiation**
> **Support:** Limit the number of headings you expect children to include.
>
> **Extension:** The children can use their table to write a paragraph outlining the main similarities and differences.

2. Paved with gold

> **Objective**
> To use inference to make comparisons backed by evidence.
>
> **What you need**
> Copies of *Windrush Child*, Extract 1.
>
> **Cross-curricular links**
> History, geography

What to do

- Read Extract 1 together. Ask: *How did the posters advertise Britain?* (easy money, good jobs, welcoming) *Why did Britain encourage people from Jamaica?* (It needed help rebuilding after the war; Jamaica was part of the British Empire, they were British citizens, they learned about Britain in school and spoke English.) Ask: *Why did Leonard's father go to Britain?* (He had to support his family – struggled to provide by selling fruit and vegetables.) *What was his plan?* (Earn enough to return and have a better life in Jamaica.) *How did it work out?* (He became a bus driver, sent for family after ten years, little extra money.)

- In groups, ask children to read Chapters 10 to 12, making notes on Leonard's family's life when they arrived. Ask: *How did their lives compare to how Leonard's father thought it would be? How was it different from what Leonard expected?* Ask volunteers to summarise their ideas.

- Read Chapter 17 from 'Let me tell you something' to the end. Ask: *Does this change your view on Britain being a good place to come to?*

- Ask groups to design a poster showing what Britain was really like for immigrants like Leonard and his family in those days, using images and slogans.

> **Differentiation**
> **Support:** Provide groups with ideas for their poster: cold, shared accommodation, racism, not welcome, welfare state.
>
> **Extension:** Ask children to make a poster on what life was really like in Jamaica.

3. Growing, changing and developing

Objective
To analyse how authors build characters.

What you need
Copies of *Windrush Child*, photocopiable page 29 'Growing, changing and developing'.

What to do

- Initiate a discussion on how we change as we grow up. Ask: *How are you different now compared with when you started school?* Encourage the children to think about different types of changes. Write these categories on the board as a guide: 'Physical', 'Attitudes', 'Character', 'Friends', 'Likes and dislikes', 'Experiences', 'Knowledge'.

- Ask: *How does the author show Leonard changing though the book?* (Through what he enjoys, people who are important to him, how he reacts to situations, how his attitudes change and so on.) Discuss how authors build characters. Books rarely explicitly say what a character is like. Readers infer this knowledge through a character's actions, thoughts and what they say.

- Hand out copies of photocopiable page 29 'Growing, changing and developing'. Ask: *What details illustrate Leonard changing?* Explain that they won't find information on all the categories listed on the board at each stage of his life, but small details here and there build the picture. Model a few examples, such as at 16, he enjoys dancing and music.

- Give time to complete the activity, either with the children skimming through the book at the end or as an ongoing activity as they progress through the book. Share their findings together at the end.

Differentiation
Support: Allow children to work in groups, with each child focusing on a different stage of Leonard's life.

Extension: Ask children to make notes on how Leonard's dad changed through the book.

4. Time passing

Objective
To discuss books that are structured in different ways.

What you need
Copies of *Windrush Child*, photocopiable page 30 'Time passing'.

Cross-curricular link
History

What to do

- Revise the standard story structure in fiction texts. Ask: *What are the main stages in a standard fiction story?* (introduction, complication/challenge, build-up, climax, resolution, conclusion)

- Invite the children to suggest important events in the story. This activity can be done to review the book or as an ongoing activity. Gather initial ideas on the board. Hand out copies of photocopiable page 30 'Time passing' and ask the children to complete it, independently, in pairs or in groups, skimming the book for further key events. Guide them with questions, for example: *Around when did Leonard likely retire?* (Probably 2012/2013, when he reached retirement age.) Exact dates/years are not necessary for everything, but they should try to sequence events correctly, marking them roughly on the timeline.

- Ask: *How does the plot differ from the standard story structure?* (No single complication/build-up/climax, instead it has many significant events; no resolution or conclusion.) Ask: *Why did the author leave the ending unclear?* (It reflects modern events, with similar situations that remain unresolved for people of the Windrush generation.) Discuss how the end links to the prologue and survey whether the children enjoyed this ending. Ask: *If the narrator had been a real person, what genre would the book be?* (autobiography)

Differentiation
Support: Select specific events for the children to plot on the timeline.

Extension: Ask children to write a brief summary of the book based on the timeline.

5. Important people

Objective

To infer characters' feelings, thoughts and motives from their actions, and justify inferences with evidence.

What you need

Copies of *Windrush Child*, photocopiable page 31 'Important people'.

What to do

- As a class, identify important characters in Leonard's life (Grandma, Brother Book, Mum, Dad, Winston, Mick, Anna, Grace – possibly Mark, Michael and Rosie, Shirley, Maud). Organise the children into groups and allocate a character to each group. More than one group can work on a character. Ask groups to discuss what they know about their character and relationship with Leonard.

- Write on the board: 'Physical characteristics' (colour, age and so on), 'Personality' (what they are like), 'Important events/actions' (how their lives are connected). Ask groups to create a mind map for their character based on these criteria, before collecting adjectives to describe their character to add to the mind map. Invite groups who looked at the same characters to share ideas. Ask: *What effect or influence did your character have on Leonard?* Ask groups to summarise their ideas, using evidence from the text and their notes to support their ideas.

- Now invite a spokesperson for each character to summarise their character, following the criteria on the board, and outline how their character linked to Leonard and whether he/she was a positive or negative influence on him and why. Remind them to support their ideas with detail from the text. Allow time for questions and comment from the class.

Differentiation

Support: Give groups page references to help children find information about their character.

Extension: Groups can summarise more than one character using photocopiable page 31 'Important people'.

6. Beginning and ending

Objective

To investigate beginnings and endings.

What you need

Copies of *Windrush Child*.

Cross-curricular links

History, PSHE

What to do

- Do this activity before reading the final chapter. Discuss how fiction stories usually begin. Ask: *What does a book's introduction usually include?* (Setting scene; introducing key characters.) Invite volunteers to say how their independent reading books begin and if they follow the pattern.

- Re-read the *Windrush Child* prologue. Ask: *What do you think of this beginning? How is it different to a usual beginning?* (Very short; doesn't set scene or seem to introduce Leonard – the protagonist mentioned on the cover.) Ask: *Who do you think the old man is? Why?* (They may guess it is Leonard as an old man.)

- Find out whether the children have read any other books with a prologue. If so, ask: *How did the prologue link to the rest of the story?* Remind them that prologues can relate to a point before, during or after the story. Ask: *When do you think this prologue is set?* (after)

- Before reading the final chapter, ask: *What do you think will happen next?* Note ideas on the board. Read the final chapter of the story together. Ask: *How does the end link to the prologue?* (The prologue foreshadows what happens to Leonard when he tries to go to Jamaica.) Ask: *Were there any clues in the story to this ending?* (Leonard not having a passport as a record of entering Britain legally.)

Differentiation

Support: Provide children with questions to help them analyse their book's introduction. Ask: *What characters are mentioned? What is the setting? What happens?*

Extension: Ask children to research the Windrush scandal and write a paragraph predicting what happens to Leonard next.

7. Pivotal moments

> **Objective**
> To explore the pivotal moments in the novel.
> **What you need**
> Copies of *Windrush Child*.
> **Cross-curricular link**
> PSHE

What to do

- Begin by asking: *What is a pivotal moment?* (an important or critical time) Have a class discussion about pivotal moments in our own lives. Share examples from your life, such as when you left school or started your first job. Explain why it was such an important moment. Invite volunteers to share their pivotal moments, guiding them to explore why those moments were so important with questions.

- Revise how the *Windrush Child* plot differs from standard fiction (no single complication/build-up/climax; no conclusion). Ask: *What were the pivotal moments in Leonard's life? Why were these events so important?* (Many events could be chosen: moving to England, playing soccer with his dad, Grandma dying, starting secondary school, his mum leaving, his talk with Dad about the welfare state, leaving school and starting work, getting beaten up, Dad dying, meeting Gracie, Mum returning to Jamaica, being detained – each event changed Leonard's attitude or understanding about his life as an immigrant.)

- Ask the children, in pairs, to choose a pivotal moment in Leonard's life and develop an interview role play around it, using cards for notes. One person interviews Leonard as his biographer, finding out important events in his life and why they were important; the other is Leonard, responding. Invite volunteers to perform their role plays.

> **Differentiation**
> **Support:** Provide pairs with the interviewer's questions.
>
> **Extension:** Ask pairs to 'interview' other characters about pivotal moments in their lives.

8. Identifying themes

> **Objective**
> To analyse the novel's themes.
> **What you need**
> Copies of *Windrush Child*.

What to do

- Ask: *What is a theme in a story?* (A unifying idea that occurs throughout.) Discuss well-known stories (traditional or fairy tales, fables) and invite children to identify themes in them, for example, good overcomes evil, good deeds are rewarded, a moral lesson and so on. Now, invite the children to discuss their independent reading books and identify common themes (friendship, loyalty, love, courage, family, growing up, belonging/identity, jealousy, anger, suffering or even a moral lesson such as 'bullying is wrong'). Encourage the children to use evidence from their books. Explain that themes are not explicit, they have to be inferred from events or a characters' words and actions as they respond to situations.

- Ask: *What themes can you identify in* Windrush Child*?* (friendship, loyalty, identity/belonging, racism, betrayal, perseverance) Choose two or three to write on the board. Ask: *What made you think of this theme?* If necessary, model using evidence to support ideas. For example, friendship: friends were important in Leonard's life, such as Fred, who taught him a trade, gave advice, and shared experiences about life, history and love of reggae. Populate mind maps on the board with evidence supporting each theme, demonstrating how the theme is inferred.

- Ask the children to choose a theme from the board and write a paragraph explaining how that theme is reflected in the book.

> **Differentiation**
> **Support:** Provide the evidence for one of the themes to use in their paragraph.
>
> **Extension:** Encourage the children to write about more than one theme.

Growing, changing and developing

- Scan the book for details that build Leonard's character at different stages in his life. Use key words instead of complete sentences.

Leonard in Jamaica	Leonard travelling
	Upset about no passport

Leonard at primary school in England	Leonard at secondary school

Leonard after school (16+)	Leonard at 71
Enjoys music and dancing	

Time passing

- Plot important events in Leonard's life on to the timeline. Plot events above and below the line.
- Add exact dates if you know them.

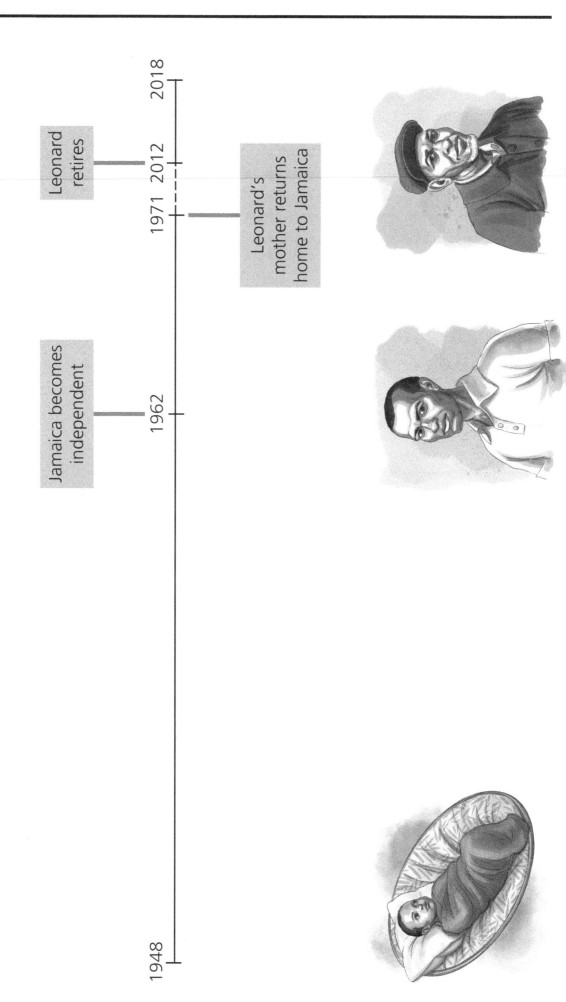

1948

Jamaica becomes independent

1962

Leonard's mother returns home to Jamaica

1971 2012

Leonard retires

2018

Important people

- Make notes on the important people in Leonard's life. Use key words.

Name: Physical characteristics: Personality: Important events/actions: Influence on Leonard: Adjectives:	**Name:** Physical characteristics: Personality: Important events/actions: Influence on Leonard: Adjectives:
Name: Physical characteristics: Personality: Important events/actions: Influence on Leonard: Adjectives:	**Name:** Physical characteristics: Personality: Important events/actions: Influence on Leonard: Adjectives:

TALK ABOUT IT ▶

1. Take the stage

Objective

To participate in drama with opportunities to improvise.

What you need

Copies of *Windrush Child*, basic props for acting out.

What to do

- Find out who enjoys live theatre, which plays they've watched and what they enjoy about it. Let the children relate their own experiences.

- Ask: *Who likes to perform in front of others?* Find out what they like or dislike about performing.

- Discuss the benefits of acting out a scene from a book such as *Windrush Child*. (You get to understand the story better and imagine how the characters felt.)

- Together, make a list of scenes from the story that might be good to act out – usually those with interesting dialogue or context. Choose volunteers to read them aloud. Ask: *How can scenes be adapted for acting? Will the dialogue change or be improvised? What props could be used?*

- Organise groups according to the scene they choose, and the number of characters needed.

- Write a list of criteria on the board to guide them as they practise their scene. For example: face the audience, speak clearly and in character, use facial expressions and body language.

- Invite each group to perform in front of the class. Afterwards have a feedback session where the children express how they felt about playing the characters and acting in front of an audience.

Differentiation

Support: Let groups prepare 'an audio' of the scene by reading aloud with expression.

Extension: Create a new scene for groups to perform, unprepared, with improvised dialogue.

2. Lions roar

Objective

To develop understanding by exploring ideas.

What you need

Copies of *Windrush Child*, photocopiable page 35 'Lions roar'.

What to do

- Together, read Chapter 5 from 'Then I went to my grandma and held her hand…' to 'She was very matter of fact'. Ask: *What advice does she give Leonard? What does she mean? Why does she think Leonard needs this advice?*

- Write these words on the board and invite children to look them up and discuss their meaning: 'infer', 'imply', 'deduce' (the speaker implies… the listener infers/deduces from it…).

- Organise small discussion groups. Briefly revise rules for a discussion and write reminders on the board, for example: take turns to speak, don't shout over and above others, be polite – use phrases such as 'I disagree because…'.

- Hand out photocopiable page 35 'Lions roar'. Ask the children to discuss the questions provided and make notes. Their notes should summarise their thoughts and opinions and include other points of view. Afterwards, each group chooses a spokesperson to report to the class.

- End with a short discussion about the kind of advice children have been given by adults. Find out what they think about the advice and if they choose to follow it. Ask them to explain why.

Differentiation

Support: Let children work together to answer the questions, discuss and make notes.

Extension: Choose a new extract (or dilemma) from the story, and have children design their own discussion questions using the words 'imply', 'infer' and 'deduce'.

3. Sticks and stones

Objective
To speak audibly and fluently.

What you need
Copies of *Windrush Child*.

Cross-curricular link
PSHE

What to do

- Write the following expression on the board: 'sticks and stones may break my bones but words will never hurt me'. Discuss its meaning (link it to social media and discuss how people hurt or bully each other online with their words). Ask: *Would Leonard have agreed with this expression?* Skim the story for examples where he was hurt by words.

- Write other expressions on the board: 'actions speak louder than words', 'empty words', 'give your word', 'to have the last word', 'be someone of your word', 'spread the word', 'a picture is worth a thousand words'. In pairs or small groups, let the children discuss the meaning of these expressions and report back to the class.

- Invite the children to prepare a speech on 'The power of words' using an expression that inspires them to speak with conviction. Provide some sentence stems as support, such as: 'Without a doubt…', 'It is vital that…', 'In conclusion…'.

- Revise speech format: introduction (to gain the audience's attention), body (provide two or three good points and examples), conclusion (end with a strong statement or quote to summarise your message). Also revise important tips for presenting a speech, such as eye contact and volume.

- Invite children to list criteria for a good speech. Allow them time to write their speeches, practise with a partner and present to the class. Children can assess each other using their list of criteria.

Differentiation

Support: Ask children to make a poster of their chosen expression and present it to the class.

Extension: Tell children to write an extended speech and present it to a larger audience, such as in assembly or at parents' evening.

4. Explore genre

Objective
To explain their understanding of genres.

What you need
Examples of different genres including historical fiction, Extract 4.

What to do

- If possible, display examples of historical fiction and non-fiction books. Ask: *How are they similar yet different?* (Usually, the setting and context is real, sometimes the characters are real, but the story is made-up. Sometimes, to find out, you should read what the author has to say about it.)

- Invite the children to explain why *Windrush Child* is historical fiction (the context and setting is real, but the character is a fictional character with experiences based on the author's and others' experiences). Read Extract 4 and identify the historical and geographical setting.

- In groups, invite the children to discuss these questions: *Do you enjoy this genre? Is there another genre you prefer? What other genres do you read for enjoyment? What genre do you not enjoy?*

- Ask the children to share their reading books with the class. Together, discuss and categorise books according to their genre. Ask: *Which is your favourite genre? Have you tried a new genre lately?*

- The children make posters to promote *Windrush Child* as a historical fiction book. (Alternatively, their poster could focus on promoting historical fiction as a genre and present various examples of age-appropriate books.)

Differentiation

Support: Start a class poster of different genres. Display it and encourage the children to add their examples to the poster.

Extension: Suggest other historical fiction books for the children to read and review.

5. Step into someone else's shoes

Objective

To adopt, create and sustain a role and respond appropriately to others in role.

What you need

Copies of the book *Windrush Child*, photocopiable page 36 'Step into someone else's shoes'.

What to do

- Together, read Chapter 10. Discuss how Leonard felt about meeting his dad for the first time since he was a baby and seeing his new home. (Leonard felt like he didn't know his dad, he was disappointed with what he saw, he didn't think it looked like a better life.) Ask: *What could have helped Leonard understand the situation better?* (communicating with his dad before he got there)

- Invite the children to imagine a conversation between Leonard and his dad using a phone or a computer to speak to each other. Discuss questions that Leonard could have asked his dad about life in England. (Do you like it there? What is your job? Have you made friends? What kind of house do you have? Why aren't you coming back to Jamaica?)

- Revise the difference between closed and open questions. (Closed questions require specific information, open questions require opinion and further detail.) Hand out photocopiable page 36 'Step into someone else's shoes'. In pairs, the children discuss and write their own open and closed questions.

- Role play a telephone conversation with characters talking in the first person.

Differentiation

Support: Provide example questions for Leonard to ask his dad – closed and open.

Extension: Ask children to retell an event from a character's perspective, for example, Mum talking about the day she and Leonard left for Jamaica.

6. A better life?

Objective

To articulate and justify opinions.

What you need

Copies of *Windrush Child*, photocopiable page 37 'A better life?'.

What to do

- Write the words 'better life' on the board. Invite the children to explain what it means to have a better life. Ask: *Is a 'better life' the same for everyone?* (No, everyone has different contexts, goals and dreams.) *Did Leonard want a 'better life'?* (No, he was happy staying with his grandma in Jamaica, he didn't know anything 'better'.)

- Hand out the photocopiable page 37 'A better life?'. Invite the children to discuss with a partner the pros and cons of Leonard and his family staying in Jamaica and the pros and cons of them moving to England.

- Invite the children to discuss the question: *Based on the pros and cons, do you think Leonard's dad gave him a better life by taking him to England?* Or, *Did Leonard have a better life in England than he would have had in Jamaica?* Provide stems to assist and support the discussion, such as: 'I agree but…', 'I disagree because…', 'Your point is good and I think…', 'I would like to add…'.

- Individually, the children write a short paragraph expressing their point of view and then share it.

- If time permits, hold a class discussion on the question: *Did Leonard's dad do the right thing by taking his family to England?*

Differentiation

Support: Explain the meaning of 'pros and cons'. Relate it to a familiar context, such as the pros and cons of homework or having an older sibling or being 11 years old.

Extension: Invite children to debate another dilemma from the story.

Lions roar

- Read Grandma's advice in Chapter 5.

- In groups, discuss the questions, make notes and report back.

1. What was Grandma's advice to Leonard?

_____

2. Why did she think Leonard needed this advice?

_____

3. What did her advice imply about her own experience?

_____

4. Do you think it was good advice for Leonard? Why?

_____

5. Does Leonard take the advice? Explain.

_____

6. Do Leonard's parents take her advice? Explain.

_____

7. What does Leonard infer from this?

_____

8. What advice do Leonard's parents give him later on?

_____

9. What does Leonard deduce (conclude) from this?

_____

10. What advice have you been given by adults in your life? Do you think it's good advice? Do you think you need it? Why?

_____

Step into someone else's shoes

- Work in pairs. Write questions Leonard could have asked his dad before arriving in England. Write his dad's answers.

- Include open and closed questions.

Leonard's question: _____

_____

Dad's answer: _____

_____

Leonard's question: _____

_____

Dad's answer: _____

_____

Leonard's question: _____

_____

Dad's answer: _____

_____

Leonard's question: _____

_____

Dad's answer: _____

_____

Leonard's question: _____

_____

Dad's answer: _____

_____

A better life?

- Discuss the pros and cons of staying in Jamaica for Leonard and his family.
- Discuss the pros and cons of the family moving to England.

Pros of staying in Jamaica	Cons of staying in Jamaica
Pros of moving to England	**Cons of moving to England**

- Based on the pros and cons, do you think Leonard's family should have moved to England? Make notes to explain your view.

_____

_____

_____

GET WRITING ▶

1. Another land

Objective
To use organisational and presentational devices to structure text.

What you need
Copies of *Windrush Child*, Extract 4, poster board.

What to do

- Together, skim Extract 4. Ask the children to identify (a) the type of text (factual, non-fiction) and (b) the organisational features used to create an interesting, eye-catching information page that is appealing and easy to read. List them on the board. Identify and link the audience, purpose, language and layout of the text.

- Ask: *Did Leonard know much about England before he got there? If you were Leonard, what would you have wanted to know about your new home? What information would have been helpful?* Invite the children to make a mind map of topics that Leonard could have researched about England before he arrived (geographical setting, weather, main cities, important ports, currency, festivals and holidays, main historic events, politics, and so on).

- Invite the children to imagine moving to a new country they know little about. They may choose Jamaica or one of the other Caribbean islands, or they may choose any other country that interests them. Make a mind map of information about this country using the headings suggested above. Discuss ideas for organising the information.

- Children create and present a well-structured project board with headings and sections.

Differentiation
Support: Provide information in class so the children don't have to do independent research.

Extension: Ask children to create a travel brochure to promote the area, listing things to do and places to see.

2. Message in a bottle

Objective
To show awareness of the audience, purpose and context.

What you need
Copies of *Windrush Child*, photocopiable page 41 'Message in a bottle'.

What to do

- Begin by asking: *What is 'a message in a bottle'?* (A form of communication, traditionally a letter or note placed in a sealed bottle and cast out to sea, the message may or may not be addressed to a real or imaginary person, it may be a call for help, a tribute to someone, a memory of someone, or even a scientific study/experiment.)

- Read Chapter 7. Invite the children to imagine Leonard sending a message in a bottle. Ask: *Who would he write to? What would he want them to know? What request might he make?* Consider the context, the purpose and the audience. (The audience could be a specific person, or a stranger.)

- Write some starter ideas on the board: 'By the time you find this message I'll be a long way from home…', 'If you find this message, please give it to…', 'I hope this message makes it home…'.

- Hand out photocopiable page 41 'Message in a bottle'. Ask children to use it to plan, edit then write out the message.

- When finished, invite the children to read aloud their messages.

Differentiation
Support: Write relevant vocabulary on the board as requested by the children.

Extension: Challenge children to change the audience, purpose and context of the message, for example, send a message to outer space or bury it in a time capsule.

3. Dialogue

Objective

To write dialogue to convey character.

What you need

Copies of *Windrush Child*, Extract 3.

What to do

- Read together Extract 3. Highlight the dialogue and discuss how it matches the characters. Ask: *Is the dialogue formal or informal? How would you describe it – is it confrontational, friendly or agreeable? What does this dialogue tell you about the characters and their situation?*

- Find other examples of dialogue in the story. Describe the characters and setting. Discuss how the author uses dialogue between the characters to imply things such as age, position in the family, attitude toward each other and the tone of the conversation.

- Invite the children to think of situations where dialogue can be integrated into the story (Leonard and Winston meeting on the ship, Leonard and his dad chatting on the bus, Leonard's dad and mum discussing when to tell Leonard about his grandma passing).

- Revise rules for punctuation in dialogue and write them on the board (a new speaker begins on a new line, inverted commas indicate the spoken words, linking narrative comes before or after, capitals and other punctuation are included inside the inverted commas).

- Children work in pairs to discuss ideas for their dialogue. They can plan it together and share ideas. Check that their dialogue conveys character.

- Tell children to write and edit their dialogue individually before proofreading each other's work.

Differentiation

Support: Ask children to create a cartoon with dialogue in speech bubbles.

Extension: Invite children to extend the dialogue with descriptions of the characters and the setting.

4. My story

Objective

To write narratives.

What you need

Copies of *Windrush Child*.

What to do

- Draw an example timeline on the board with a start and end date and two or three key dates in between. Ask: *Where have you seen or used timelines?* (History) *What is their purpose?* (provides key information, summarises a period chronologically)

- Discuss key events in Leonard's life. Read some extracts aloud. Discuss the style and tone of the text (narrative, personal perspective, honest, detailed, first person).

- Ask the children to work individually to create a timeline of key events in their own lives. Afterwards, invite them to sit in pairs and share the information.

- Tell the children to write a narrative (a story) of their life so far including setting and characters. Ask: *Where will your story take place? Who will you include? What events will you mention?* Give ideas for a good beginning: 'The first thing I remember…', 'My mum once told me that the day I was born…', 'Much to everyone's surprise, my first words were…'.

- Encourage the children to use the same style and tone as the book. Write words from the Years 5 and 6 word list on the board for them to include in their story, for example, 'according', 'achieve', 'apparent', 'curiosity', 'determined', 'develop', 'excellent', 'existence'.

- Give children time to plan, edit and write a final draft. Let children read their stories to each other in small groups.

Differentiation

Support: Let children write one paragraph only and assist with the editing process.

Extension: Challenge children to write as many paragraphs as possible, including dialogue.

5. Report it

Objective
To identify the audience and purpose and use appropriate forms of writing.

What you need
Copies of *Windrush Child*, Extract 4, examples of newspaper articles, photocopiable page 42 'Report it'.

What to do
- Write these words on the board: 'audience', 'purpose', 'language' and 'layout'. Discuss how they link (every text has a purpose and an audience – this determines the language and layout).

- Discuss the audience, purpose, language and layout of *Windrush Child*. Compare and analyse other text examples (letters, postcards, magazines, newspapers).

- Read Extract 4. When the first people arrived from Jamaica and the Caribbean, reporters were there to interview the passengers and report the story. The news made the headlines. Think of ideas for headlines ('Help is here!', 'Welcome aboard!', 'Welcome Windrush', 'All hands on deck!', 'They've made it').

- Tell children to use the information in Extract 4 (and research other information if necessary) to write a news article about the arrival, as if they were there. Recall the structure of a news article. Remind children to focus on the 'who, what, where, when, why and how' of the story in the first paragraph, followed by less important details.

- Hand out photocopiable page 42 'Report it'. Ask children to plan, edit and then write their final draft on to A4 pages. Display them in class.

Differentiation
Support: Let children focus on the headline and first paragraph only.

Extension: Children can choose a different event mentioned in the story and write a news report (such as when Leonard's dad crashed his bus in Chapter 26 or when they celebrated Jamaican Independence Day in Chapter 25).

6. Book review

Objective
To summarise the story.

What you need
Copies of *Windrush Child*, examples of book reviews, photocopiable page 43 'Book review', Years 5 and 6 word list.

What to do
- Collect examples of book reviews that the children will enjoy. In small groups, provide copies and invite the children to read and discuss these reviews. Write questions on the board about *Windrush Child* to guide the discussion: 'Is the review formal or informal?', 'Does it have a specific format?', 'Who wrote it?', 'Is it positive or negative?', 'What information does it include about the book and the story?'

- Discuss the purpose of a review (to summarise the plot, giving the audience enough detail to help them decide if they want to read the book, without giving away the ending).

- In pairs, invite the children to summarise each chapter in one or two phrases. They should swap partners and share ideas. Explain that they will use these ideas to write their own plot summary.

- Hand out photocopiable page 43 'Book review' to guide children's thinking and planning. Remind them to use the correct format and style, and to summarise the plot skilfully without giving away the end.

- Display some words from the Years 5 and 6 word list. Encourage the children to use them in their review: 'appreciate', 'controversy', 'foreign', 'harass', 'identify', 'individual', 'opportunity', 'prejudice'.

Differentiation
Support: Invite children to work in pairs to make a poster review of the book to promote it.

Extension: Challenge children to present a book review as a multimedia presentation with audio recordings of key extracts.

Message in a bottle

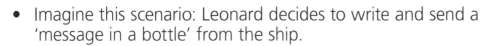

- Imagine this scenario: Leonard decides to write and send a 'message in a bottle' from the ship.

- Plan, edit and then write his message here. (You can then cut it out and place it in a bottle!)

Report it

- Write a headline about the arrival of the *Empire Windrush* then report the story as if you were there, interviewing the passengers.

The Tilbury Times

Book review

- Write an honest review of the book. Include important details, a summary of the plot and what you thought about it.

Important details

Title	
Author	
Publisher	
Genre	
Age level	
Themes	

Main characters (with a short description or extract)

Plot summary

_____

_____

_____

_____

_____

_____

- Rate the book and say who you think might enjoy it.   ☆ ☆ ☆ ☆ ☆

_____

_____

ASSESSMENT ▶

1. Making friends

Objectives
To listen and respond appropriately; to summarise the main ideas.

What you need
Copies of *Windrush Child*.

What to do

- Ask the children: *Did Leonard find it difficult to make friends in England? Why?*

- Write the following words and phrases on the board and discuss their meaning: 'relate', 'identify', 'common ground', 'in the same boat'.

- Tell the children you are going to read an extract from the story. Invite them to focus on the text by either closing their eyes, putting their heads down or looking at the reader. Write some question words on the board ('who', 'what', 'where', 'when', 'why') as a reminder of the details to notice.

- Read Chapter 17 from the beginning to '"They don't even like us here," I replied, "And it's so cold".' Check their understanding by asking: *Whom does Leonard meet? What makes them different or the same? Why does Leonard feel comfortable with them?*

- Read the extract again. Remind the children to listen for details (and make notes if necessary).

- Invite the children to do one of the following activities in response to the text: list the events in order with as much detail as possible, or summarise the extract in a paragraph using their own words. Assess their ability to listen for information and demonstrate their understanding.

Differentiation
Support: Ask children to create a mind map with key words to remember the details as they listen.

Extension: Tell children to write five questions about the extract, then swap questions and answer them.

2. Dear Grandma

Objective
To distinguish between the language of speech and writing and choose the appropriate register.

What you need
Copies of *Windrush Child*.

What to do

- Read Chapter 11 to the end of the letter from Leonard's grandma. Discuss why letters are less popular now than in the past (we use other ways to communicate, such as emails and social media). Ask: *How long did her letter take to arrive? When did Leonard receive it?*

- Recall register (different styles of speaking and writing). Compare the letter's register to their conversations. Ask: *How is it different? Does Grandma sound different compared with how she usually spoke to Leonard? What was her tone? Why did she use capital letters?* (Maybe she felt it looked more important.)

- Invite children to work in small groups to imagine Leonard's reply. Ask them to recall details to develop a mind map of things to tell his grandma about England. Use headings: 'Food', 'Weather', 'Transport', 'Home', 'School', 'Friends', 'Family'.

- Identify the register Leonard might use in his letter. Ask: *Is writing to an adult similar or different to writing to a friend? Is it different if the adult is a family member?* (Communication is either formal or informal depending on how familiar people are.)

- Ask the children to independently plan and write a letter from Leonard to his grandma focusing on the style, tone and content.

Differentiation
Support: Ask children to write a brief letter or postcard from Leonard to Grandma.

Extension: Introduce a different scenario – let children write a letter from Leonard's mum or dad to Grandma.

3. Make links

Objective
To link ideas within and across sentences and paragraphs.

What you need
Copies of *Windrush Child*.

Cross-curricular link
PSHE

What to do

- Begin a short discussion by asking: *Was Leonard happy in England?* Suggest that the answer could be 'yes', 'no' or 'both' and ask children to recall key aspects from the story to support this. (Leonard was unhappy initially but later he began to enjoy aspects of his life in England.)

- Ask children to recall what they know about conjunctions. Discuss how they can be used to create cohesion. Conjunctions ('but', 'and', 'for', 'yet', 'so', 'although', 'because', 'therefore', 'however' and so on) link words/sentences/ clauses/paragraphs to show contrast, addition, consequence and so on, such as 'Leonard loved his parents yet he missed his grandma.' Adverbials can indicate time and place, such as 'At first, Leonard was unhappy in England, but he settled down eventually.' Skim the story for examples of cohesive devices creating links.

- Ask the children to write a paragraph describing Leonard's feelings at different moments, explaining his battle to settle in a new place and be happy. Their paragraph structure should include a beginning, a middle and an end. Remind them to focus on using conjunctions and adverbials to make links within and between sentences. Assess their ability to write coherently, linking ideas and events so that their writing flows and makes sense.

Differentiation

Support: Provide sentence stems as a frame: 'In 1958...', 'At first...', 'Although he enjoyed...', 'Later on...', 'He was heartbroken when...', 'In 1962, they celebrated because...'.

Extension: Ask children to write several paragraphs to show how to link ideas across paragraphs.

4. Culture and customs

Objective
To participate in presentations.

What you need
Pictures, posters or books on other cultures, traditions and customs.

Cross-curricular links
Geography, PSHE

What to do

- Write the words 'culture' and 'customs' on the board. Provide definitions using everyday language (culture – the common ideas and customs of a particular group of people; custom, also called tradition – a common behaviour passed down through generations within a group of people, including ceremonies, celebrations, festivals, meals, clothes, beliefs, music). Ask: *What traditions do your family enjoy?*

- When Leonard arrived in England, he faced another culture and different customs. Recall and discuss the challenges of fitting in and leaving behind the things he was used to (food, clothes, general way of life).

- In small groups, ask the children to choose a country or culture to research. Write a list of ideas on the board. Children may choose a culture mentioned in *Windrush Child*, their own culture, that of someone in their group, or a country and culture they've heard about or are interested in.

- Ask groups to prepare a presentation. Encourage them to include traditional clothes, food and ceremonies or celebrations. Each child in the group should have a role in the group (director, scribe and so on) and have a turn to speak.

Differentiation

Support: Provide all information in class for research.

Extension: Extend the activity to other classes and include the school in a 'Culture and Customs Day'.

5. A way with words

Objective

To spell and use words accurately.

What you need

Copies of *Windrush Child*, Years 5 and 6 word list, dictionaries, thesauruses.

What to do

- Begin by asking the children if they find the story easy or difficult to read. Ask: *Why? Is the language and vocabulary simple or challenging? Which words did you find difficult? Why do you think this is so?* (narrator uses simple, child-like language and vocabulary while dealing with challenging and complex issues, making it accessible to younger readers)

- Write the following words on the board: 'harass', 'foreign', 'sacrifice'. Explain that these words might not be used in the story but they relate to it. Provide child-speak definitions, then ask the children to find dictionary definitions and then use them in sentences of their own. Highlight tricky spelling patterns and sounds.

- Write further words from the Years 5 and 6 word list on the board: 'achieve', 'appreciate', 'communicate', 'community', 'correspond', 'equip'/'equipped', 'familiar'/'unfamiliar', 'hindrance', 'identify', 'opportunity' and so on.

- In pairs, children can use dictionaries to look up the meaning of the words and then practise spelling the words correctly, taking turns to test each other. Invite volunteers to share strategies for remembering tricky spellings.

- Ask children to work individually to choose words related to the story to use in sentences of their own, explaining some of the issues and dilemmas the story addresses.

Differentiation

Support: Limit the number of words and let children use dictionaries to find the meaning of these words.

Extension: Ask children to use thesauruses to find two synonyms for each word.

6. Read for meaning

Objective

To understand what they read.

What you need

Copies of *Windrush Child*, photocopiable page 47 'Read for meaning'.

What to do

- Open by explaining that the children are going to do a comprehension activity. Set the scene. Ask: *Why did it take so long for Leonard to settle in England? What did he find the most difficult? What advice did his parents give him? Was it helpful?* Invite their responses, without providing any specific answers or conclusions.

- Prepare the children for the comprehension activity. Revise general comprehension techniques: reading the questions carefully, analysing lower order questions (an explicit answer from the text) and higher order questions (inference required to answer), skimming the text for context and clues, scanning for details and specific information, checking the meaning of unfamiliar words in context, re-reading the questions and text before answering in full sentences.

- Together, read from '"Come with me," Dad said,' in Chapter 17 to the end of Chapter 18. Hand out photocopiable page 47 'Read for meaning'. Read the instructions together and explain further if necessary. Ask the children to complete the comprehension, using *Windrush Child* for reference.

- Assess their ability to work independently, demonstrating their comprehension skills.

Differentiation

Support: Limit the number of questions children are to answer. Allow them to answer without using full sentences so they focus on the answer rather than the grammar, spelling and punctuation.

Extension: After finishing, ask the children to summarise the extract in their own words. Set word limits as appropriate.

Read for meaning

- Read from '"Come with me," Dad said,' in Chapter 17 to the end of Chapter 18.

- Answer the questions in your notebook.

1. In Chapter 17, Leonard's dad talks to him.

   a. What was the reason for their talk?

   b. What word did Leonard's dad use to describe life in Jamaica?

   c. Find an appropriate synonym for this word.

   d. What is the opposite of it? (antonym)

   e. Leonard's dad points out positive things about working and living in England. Give one example of each.

   f. What is a welfare state?

2. At the end of Chapter 17 and the beginning of Chapter 18, Leonard's attitude changes.

   a. How does his attitude begin to change?

   b. Give two examples of his actions that support this.

   c. What effect does this sentence have?

   'I was lying awake… thinking about what I was going to do when I left school when I heard Mum scream…'

3. Chapter 18 is a key event in the story.

   a. What happens to Leonard's dad in Chapter 18? Who is responsible?

   b. Why does his dad refuse to report it?

   c. What do you think Leonard's grandma would have done in this situation?

   d. What word in the text describes how Leonard felt when he sat with his injured dad?

   e. When Leonard went back to bed, did he continue to think about his future? What did he have on his mind?

   f. Explain in your own words what Leonard meant when he said: 'This is not how lions should live.'

SCHOLASTIC
READ & RESPOND

Available in this series:

978-1407-15879-2

978-1407-14224-1

978-1407-16063-4

978-1407-16056-6

978-1407-14228-9

978-1407-16069-6

978-1407-16070-2

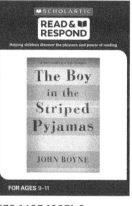
978-1407-16071-9

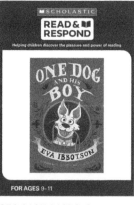
978-1407-14230-2

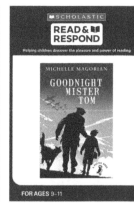
978-1407-16057-3

978-1407-16064-1

978-1407-14223-4

978-0702-30890-1

978-0702-30859-8

To find out more,
visit www.scholastic.co.uk/read-and-respond